Waiting for Dry Land
Dyslexic Friendly Edition

A Message

by

Evelyn Rainey

Copyright © 2024 Evelyn Rainey

Cover Design © 2024 Evelyn Rainey

Dyslexic Friendly Typography Copyright © 2025 Rolland Kenneson

All rights reserved. No part of this book may be reproduced, scanned, or distributed in any printed, audio or electronic form without permission. Such piracy of copyrighted materials is a violation of the author's rights and is punishable by law.

Unless otherwise indicated, all Scripture references are taken from the American Standard Version (ASV). Public Domain.

ISBN-13: 978-1-963272-07-9

ShelteringTree.Earth, LLC
PO Box 973, Eagle Lake, FL 33839
ShelteringTreeMedia.com

What is a "Dyslexic Friendly" Book?

Sheltering Tree Media has taken steps to make our books more friendly for those who live with dyslexia. While the following principles will not make every book readable for every reader, it is our best effort to create products that encourage reading and to support all readers.

Throughout the book, we use a font named OpenDyslexic. This is a free font that is designed to help dyslexic readers distinguish each letter from the others. For more information about OpenDyslexic, how it differs from other fonts, and research behind the font, visit their website: www.opendyslexic.com.

In our book created for adults, we use 12-point font. This size font provides the reader plenty of spacing between the letters (which is called kerning). The bigger, wider font tends to be easier to the reader's eyes.

The space between each word is increased (this is called word spacing). This helps better distinguish when one word ends and the next begins. The line spacing is greater than most common fonts (this is called leading). This all should help with readability.

Whenever possible, the text is Left-Aligned but it is not justified on the right side. Allowing the right side of a paragraph to remain rough keeps the word spacing consistent throughout.

Our Dyslexic Friendly books are printed on cream or ivory paper which is also thicker than the average book page. This minimizes the sharp contrast of black-on-white pages as well as bleedthrough of text from the previous page.

Finally, Sheltering Tree Media has made colored overlays available when you purchase a book through our online store. You can find these overlays at ShelteringTreeMedia.com/shop/dyslexic-friendly.

These are some of the principles we use to create a book as readable as possible to those living with dyslexia. Some may find this helpful; some may not. Please provide us with any insights you might have to improve our Dyslexic Friendly principles. We pray this will enable many to heighten their love for reading.

DEDICATION

For all those who are too terrified or too bone-weary to leave their despair behind. You can; you must. And God will help you begin again.

Pastoral Prayer

Dearest God, Utmost Divine, Holy Spirit, and Jesus the Christ,

We come today to praise your name and worship at your feet.

We ask you, Lord, to give us what we need: food, shelter, a place to belong, loved ones, and most importantly, a purpose in your kingdom. We ask for peace within our souls as we stand in a world of war. We ask for the ability to confer understanding in a world divided by deceit and betrayal. We ask for empathy in a world filled with apathy.

And we ask that You forgive us for the things we have done which were wrong. We ask you to forgive us for the things we did not do which we should have done. We ask you to forgive us for being cowards when you have shown us how to live courageously without fear.

In turn, let us forgive those who have abused us, those who have betrayed us, those who have hurt us intentionally or unintentionally. We especially want to forgive those who just ignored us, as if we were not worthy of attention.

We ask for strength to face what is to come. To stand against the foe and fight for what is true and right. We know that the victory is yours – earned by your sacrifice and enjoyed by all who call on your name.

We ask especially that we learn how to leave our sorrows behind and get up to begin a new life every day. You have plans for us which we cannot do from a place of refuge.

And now, together as the body and bride of Christ, we repeat the prayer you taught us:

Our Father, which art in heaven, hollowed be your name.

Thy kingdom come; thy will be done On Earth as it is in heaven.

Give us this day our daily bread.

And forgive us our sins as we forgive those who sin against us.

And lead us not into temptation.

But deliver us from evil.

For thine is the kingdom, and the power, and the glory, forever.

Amen.

Introduction

When Noah's world was washed away, he followed God's directions. He built the ark. He gathered enough food to feed his family and his animals for a year. He acquiesced as God make an ending to what used to be. And then he accepted the truth that his world was changed forever and would never be the same again.

Build, gather, let God shut the door, and accept the truth: these are the four things you can do to help you get through the worst situations.

But God never meant for you to just sit in the ark for the rest of your life. In your deepest despair, you still have people you need to take care of. You need to let God take you through the deep waters of that despair. Once you have found dry land, you need to get out of the ark. And once you have gotten out of the ark, you need to begin a new life.

Message

1. Take Care of What You Are Entrusted With
2. Let God Steer the Boat
3. Get Out of the Ark
4. Start a New Life

Take Care of What God Has Entrusted to You

Noah sank to the lowest level of the ark, curled up into a ball, and slept through the storm. For forty days and nights, he did nothing but sleep.

No, that's not what happened.

God could have sent the animals to the highest regions of the world. Elephants know instinctively when there is going to be a tsunami and run up to the mountains. Dogs know when there's going to be an earthquake. Bees stay closer to their hives when a storm is imminent. But God sent animals to Noah for the duration of the flood.

Why?

And Noah's family was allowed to go into the ark. God could just as easily have begun a new human race with only Noah the way he did with Adam, but God didn't. He put Ham, Shem, and Japheth and their wives into the ark, and Noah's wife.

Why?

Noah could have slept through the storm, but he didn't. God had sent him people to take care of; family members who had also lost everything they'd known. God sent him animals who needed feeding and watering, and Noah had to take care of himself, too. He had to eat and drink and wash and sleep.

One of the rules that hospice workers always stressed that I should listen to was that **caregivers must take care of themselves first.** You can't take care of someone if you don't take care of yourself first.

On an airplane, the stewardess stresses that you have to put the oxygen mask on yourself before you put it on your child.

You have to eat. Why do you think people bring over food after the funeral? So you will have something to eat for the next few weeks. God had provided the food for Noah – all those things he had gathered before the flood.

You have to eat, too. You have to derive sustenance from those things you have gathered – the songs and the Scripture and the skills and the prayerful relationship with God. These are the things you gathered to help sustain you through the dark times.

Noah had people who needed him.

He had animals that would have died if Noah didn't feed and water them.

He had to clean out their stalls. Yes, sometimes after trauma, loss, or despair, we have manure that needs to be cleared out.

I'm sure Noah didn't feel like doing anything that first day. And maybe he didn't. And maybe he didn't the second day either. But we know from Scripture that Noah was a good man, so he heard the cries of the animals and the wailing of his family, and he knew he had to help. He got up and started to work. He was still in shock from what he had lost, but he worked anyway. And by working, he realized he was hungry, so he ate. And by sweating, he realized he needed to keep clean, so he bathed.

Did you know that one of the first signs of depression is the lack of personal hygiene? It just doesn't seem to matter anymore. If you sit or stand near a person who is fragrant, maybe more than a bath, that person needs a smile from you, a show of compassion, a word of hope and a promise of better days to come.

The more Noah focused on what he had to take care of right then and there, the less was the weight of his loss.

When we go through times of trauma or loss or great sorrow, we must wait until the waters recede and there is dry ground before venturing out of our place of refuge.

When we go through times of trauma or loss or great sorrow, we must wait until our sorrow has receded before venturing out into a new beginning.

It doesn't happen overnight. People expect you to get over it according to their timeline.

Don't let people push you out of the ark until the time is right.

But how long should that time of refuge be?

The duration of your time in the ark takes as long as it takes for the sorrow, the trauma, and the loss to recede.

Noah did not run out of supplies, because he had gathered all the things God had told him to gather.

If it takes you a season, or a year, or two years for your despair to recede, let it. As long as you are still nurtured and nurturing in the things God has provided you.

Don't wallow in it, or those things that you are supposed to take care of will die out.

Don't wallow in it, or those supplies you gathered to help you through this dark time will disappear, too.

Don't wallow in your sorrow and despair. Remember from the last lesson – When Everything Gets Washed Away – accept the truth of the situation. But don't wallow in it.

Be busy.
Be useful.
Lose yourself in a purpose that is greater than just your needs.

Rely on what God has provided for you and wait on God's timing for the waters to recede.

Let God Steer the Boat
God said that there was going to be a flood which would wash your world away, but not to despair.

God told you to build a safe place according to His instructions. He told you to gather an abundance of things that will sustain you while you find safety within the ark during the flood.

God provided you with people and things that would need your love and care and gave you a purpose to fulfill during the flood.

God shut the door so that you would not have to.

The rains came. The world as you knew it was washed away. And you knew you would be inside the ark until the waters receded and you found dry land again.

So, you yelled at your sons and daughters-in-law to grab the oars and start rowing! The faster you can move through the flood, the faster you'll be able to reach the dry land and have a normal life again.

No, God didn't instruct Noah to put in oar wells or rowing benches.

Sometimes some encouraging soul advises you to, "Get over it." You have my permission to tell them, "God didn't put oars in my ark."

Sometimes, when the storm washes everything away, we drop anchors and refuse to leave our location, sure that this was once the most wonderful place in the world and once the waters recede, it will be again. But it won't. Your world has been washed away. **What you knew and who you were will never be the same again.** And sometimes, the waters rise higher than the anchors are long, and our boats flounder and sink. And we are drowned along with everything else.

Noah was a smart man, obviously. And he knew that the rains fell and the waters from the deep filled up the lower places of the earth, so the dry ground was obviously going to be in THAT direction, so he raced up to the deck, grabbed the tiller, and steered the boat to the mountainous regions of the earth.

No. There was no rudder on the ark because **God steered the boat.** God knew just when and where it would be time for Noah to find dry land.

Nights were probably the worst of times, or the best of times, depending on if Noah just shut himself away from his family or if Noah sat with his family and spent time talking about what had happened, and making plans for what was to come.

You need to talk about your trauma. You need to talk about your trauma to someone you trust and love. They don't have to be a professional counselor, they can be your minister, your best friend, your child, or your journal.

But as you talk about what happened and what is to come, **don't wallow in it!** I call these the *if only's*. You cannot change your situation by wallowing in thoughts that begin with "if only." These thoughts are like little anchors you might toss out and get snagged on the flotsam of the passing debris of what used to be. The anchor holds for just a little while, but it's not dry land.

And if someone you love begins a sentence with "if only," stop them. Gently redirect them to the here and now. When you cling to thoughts of *if only*, you churn up all the things that got washed away, but you do not hold fast to them. God cannot steer your boat to dry land if you are wallowing in the *if only's*.

Noah thought he had found dry land several times, but it wasn't right. If he'd had oars or a tiller, he could have shifted the ark to what he thought was the right location, but it wasn't **God's** location. Because it wasn't just dry land that Noah needed, it was a place where Noah and his family and all those entrusted to him could begin again.

Sometimes, after loss or trauma, we grab the first piece of dry land we see. And it is totally wrong for us. It looks right, but it isn't the right place to begin again.

We have to let God steer our boats and place us in just the right location where we can start again.

Because remember, this story was not about going into an ark while the world was washed away. **It is about getting out of the ark and building a new, better, cleaner world.**

Get Out of the Ark

I'm sure one or more of Noah's children yelled, "When is this going to end?" I'm sure of it because I'm sure people asked the same thing of you. I know they asked the same thing of me.

Genesis 8:1-5 tells us:

And God remembered Noah, and all the beasts, and all the cattle that were with him in the ark: and God made a wind to pass over the earth, and the waters assuaged; ² *the fountains also of the deep and the windows of heaven were stopped, and the rain from heaven* was restrained; ³ and the waters returned from off the earth continually: and after the end of a hundred and fifty days the waters decreased. ⁴ And the ark rested in the seventh month, on the seventeenth day of the month, upon the mountains of Ararat. ⁵ And the waters decreased continually until the tenth month: in the tenth month, on the first day of the month, were the tops of the mountains seen.

    We remember the phrase *forty days and forty nights*. But that was just the duration of the rain. It was months before the waters receded enough to get out of the ark.
    Genesis 8:1 said that *God remembered Noah*. Does that mean that He had forgotten Noah as the rains raged? Does this mean that for *forty days and forty nights*, God forgot about Noah and his family and all the animals?

Did you feel like God had forgotten about you when everything was washed away?

Forty days and forty nights is not a precise duration of time. It means a very long time, but not REALLY, REALLY long, Not an EON.

I was raised in England, and the phrase a *fortnight* literally meant two weeks, but it linguistically meant anywhere between 10 days and a month. Forty days means about 6 weeks, half a season, maybe more, maybe less. But the important definition for *forty days and forty nights* is – it is as long as it takes for the rains to stop.

How long does sorrow last?

How long does it take one to heal from trauma?

How long does it take for despair to stop gnawing on your guts and let you live?

For women, it's supposed to last one year. Historically, one wears widow's weaves for a solid year, then you're done. You're ready to get married again if you're young or to go live with your children if you're old.

For a man, historically, it was supposed to be 8 months. Time enough to find a new wife – whether you are young or old.

For trauma, the farther away from the heart the injury happened, the swifter the path to healing. Supposedly, you can heal faster if you lose your fingers or toes than if you have an injury in your abdomen. It makes sense. Maybe that's why some friends recover faster from losing someone than a family member might.

It took forty days and forty nights for the rain to stop. Then it took another 150 days for the waters to begin to go down. The ark stopped moving; it found a place on which to ground itself. But it was still surrounded by water.

Then it took another three months before the tops of the mountains were visible.

So, from losing everything to seeing the tops of the mountains:

6 weeks of non-stop rain

5 months of floating

3 more months before a hope of dry land peeked over the endless waters.

That's 9 months; it didn't happen overnight.

Genesis 8:13-14 continues the timing:

[13] *And it came to pass in the six hundred and first year, in the first month, the first day of the month, the waters were dried up from off the earth: and Noah removed the covering of the ark, and looked, and, behold, the face of the ground was dried.* [14] *And in the second month, on the seven and twentieth day of the month, was the earth dry.*

Three more months before the earth was ready for Noah to get out of the ark.

If Noah had gotten out of the ark before the earth was dry, he would have drowned. He could not have planted crops. He could not have found a place of shelter. The animals in his charge could not have survived, had he given up on waiting for God and just gotten out of the ark.

Sometimes, when we recover from trauma, loss, or despair, we stay in our comfort zone. It was a terrible world before the flood. It's nice and comfy here, with people who love me and animals who need me. I can't see the sun or feel the grass between my toes, but it's safe.

Sometimes, we wait for God to open the door of the ark. Afterall, He shut the door before the flood. Why shouldn't we just wait for God? It's all in God's timing.

If He wanted me to go out into that world, He'd open the door for me.

Sometimes, we stay in our ark until all our supplies run out and all the people and things that rely on us die, too. Might as well just sit here. Everything that didn't get washed away is right here, for now. Might as well just stay where God told me to be.
But that's not what God said.

Yes, He instructed you to build a safe place and gather what you'll need to survive the flood. But He didn't expect you to live and die there. He has work for you to do!
But not until you are ready.
When your *forty days and forty nights* are over and you see that you are now surrounded by dry land, it is your decision to open the ark and get out. And then, all those you have with you can also get out of the ark and begin life anew.

The story of Noah has taught us to
1. Build
2. Gather
3. Let God close the door
4. Accept the truth
5. Take care of what you are entrusted with
6. Let God steer the boat
7. Get out of the ark

But how do you get out of the ark? How do you put aside what you once were, and what you became?

Start a New Life

You are going into a new environment; nothing will look the same. You don't even have a home. But you know what? If you can build an ark, you can build a house.

"There's no fruit on the trees and no crops in the fields yet." You know what? There's still some of those grains and fruits God told you to gather. Use those as seeds to plant the next harvest.

"But I'm too old to start again!"
You know what? *Noah was six hundred years old when the flood of waters came upon the earth.* (Genesis 7:6)
If Noah can do it at 600, you can do it at 60.

"But nothing is the same."
No, that's not true. God is the same. He is the same yesterday, today, and tomorrow. God does not change. If – and

when – your entire world gets washed away – know that God is still with you. No matter what has changed, **God hasn't changed.** So, you can do this. You can get out of the ark and start again.

For some, it's going back to church. Or finding a new church.
For others, it's joining a social group.
Some people start a new hobby.
Some people volunteer to do that ministry their pastor has been talking about.
Some people sell all they have and move away. But they begin again in that new location.

Think how Noah and his family felt when he lifted the top off the ark and saw the sun and felt the wind and smelled the fresh earth. That's nice. Some people stop there.

But once Noah got out of the ark and placed his feet on the postdiluvian soil, and looked across the land, nothing was the same for him again. He started thinking, *I'm going to pitch my tent there, and I can lead the animals down that rivulet to clean water. I can plant wheat there, and tubers there. And the children which will come to my sons and their wives can play in that field there.*

Positive thoughts. Happy – sometimes you can just start with *happy* before you can shift to joyful thoughts.

But when you do start thinking happy thoughts, don't let anyone take those away from you. Yes, you are still a widow, but you can start having happy thoughts. Yes, your business crashed and burned, but you can start having happy thoughts. Tell them, "I can have happy thoughts!"

That first night, stretched out on the new ground under the stars, Noah felt the absence of the rocking of the ship, but knew he was where God wanted him to finally wind up.

He got out of the ark to start again.

No one is a stranger to death, to loss, to mourning and grief and despair. But no one is a stranger to **joy**, either.

When everything gets washed away, we must

1. Build
2. Gather
3. Let God close the door
4. Accept the truth
5. Take care of what you are entrusted with
6. Let God steer the boat
7. Get out of the ark
8. And we must begin again.

Benediction

As you leave this sanctuary, this safe place of prayer, praise, and worship, and go into the world to begin your life anew, remember that:
Christ is with you,
Christ goes before you,
Christ supports behind you,
Christ is on your right,
Christ is on your left,
Christ will flow through you in all that you do.
Go in peace.

Hymns, Scriptures and Holy Writings

Hymn of Preparation
Leave it There, Words & Music: Charles Albert Tindley. United Methodist Hymnal #522, (The United Methodist Publishing House, Nashville) 1989.

Closing Hymn
Faith, While Trees Are Still in Blossom, Words: Anders Frostenson, 1960, trans. By Fred Kaan, 1972. Music: V. Earle Copes, 1960. United Methodist Hymnal #508, (The United Methodist Publishing House, Nashville) 1989.

Genesis 7:6
Noah was six hundred years old when the flood of waters came upon the earth.

Genesis 8:1-5
[1] And God remembered Noah, and all the beasts, and all the cattle that were with him in the ark: and God made a wind to pass over the earth, and the waters

assuaged; ² the fountains also of the deep and the windows of heaven were stopped, and the rain from heaven was restrained; ³ and the waters returned from off the earth continually: and after the end of a hundred and fifty days the waters decreased. ⁴ And the ark rested in the seventh month, on the seventeenth day of the month, upon the mountains of Ararat. ⁵ And the waters decreased continually until the tenth month: in the tenth month, on the first day of the month, were the tops of the mountains seen.

Genesis 8:13-14
¹³ And it came to pass in the six hundred and first year, in the first month, the first day of the month, the waters were dried up from off the earth: and Noah removed the covering of the ark, and looked, and, behold, the face of the ground was dried. ¹⁴ And in the second month, on the seven and twentieth day of the month, was the earth dry.

Hebrews 11:1, 7

[1] Now faith is assurance of things hoped for, a conviction of things not seen.

[7] By faith Noah, being warned of God concerning things not seen as yet, moved with godly fear, prepared an ark to the saving of his house; through which he condemned the world, and became heir of the righteousness which is according to faith.

ABOUT THE AUTHOR

Evelyn Rainey has always loved to tell stories and help others understand. As such, she is a published author and educator. But she is also the caregiver of her mother, an herb and vegetable  gardener, cat wrangler, and crochet artist. She manages **ShelteringTree.Earth, LLC Publishing** and facilitates the **United Methodist** Temple Prayer Shawl Ministry and the Senior Adults Program there, as well as serving on the SPRC. She is in the process of becoming a Licensed Local Pastor through the United Methodist Church.

After 38 years in education, Evelyn retired after having earned BS degrees and Certificates of Endorsement in Early Childhood Education, Elementary Education, Gifted Education, Integrated Middle School Curriculum, English for Speakers of Other Languages, and Journalism. She also taught all grade levels from Kindergarten through Adult and at many different facilities, including jails and teen pregnancy centers.

    Evelyn has over a dozen books published including science fiction, fantasy, historical fiction, new age urban fantasy, metaphysical and visionary, pastoral handbooks, and children's books. She currently has a list of a dozen new projects she plans to have published over the next few years. She has facilitated writer groups (and continues to do so with on-line meetings and would love you to join them (see the https://www.shelteringtreemedia.com/events). She has been guest speaker and guest author at writer conferences and conventions throughout the southeast US.

Her love of teaching has expanded into videos for book trailers, crochet lessons, meditation series, Bible studies, as well as interviews and writing lessons. (See her YouTube channel **evelynrainey4780**.)

Unable to travel as long as she remains her mother's caregiver, Evelyn is still able to conduct interviews and conferences via phone and video communication (zoom, duo, etc.) She welcomes questions and comments from her readers but prefers to be contacted initially through https://evelynrainey.com/contact.

DISCUSSION GUIDE FOR BOOK CLUBS, JOURNALING, OR PERSONAL CONTEMPLATION

Write or discuss your answers.

1. Name three people which God has entrusted to you. Explain your relationship with these people, how they came to be in your life and how their existence interacts with you in a dependent manner.

2. Name a ministry which God has entrusted to you. Explain your relationship with this ministry, how it came to be in your life and how its existence interacts with you in a dependent manner.

3. If you were to hand your responsibility over to someone else, what would their qualifications be?

_____

_____

_____

_____

_____

_____

_____

_____

_____

4. Was there a time when someone took care of you even though they had suffered a tremendous loss? How did that make you feel?

5. Do you believe you should throw yourself into a project or something you love when you are in despair? Explain your opinion.

6. In what ways do you let God control your life? How does that impact your plans?

_____

_____

_____

_____

_____

_____

_____

_____

_____

7. In what ways do you try to control your own life? How does that impact your plans?

8. Do you have a 5-year plan for your life? Describe it.

9. Explain a time when you had to develop a Plan B. What were the circumstances and the result?

10. Does our civilization encourage or discourage you to 'let God steer the boat?' How do you deal with that?

11. Describe a situation where you knew you shouldn't stay but you just couldn't leave. What happened?

12. Does God ever want you to just take refuge and not make any changes? Why or why not? Has that ever happened to you?

13. What do you think is the strongest reason NOT to get out of your place of refuge?

_____

_____

_____

_____

_____

_____

_____

_____

14. What do you think is the strongest reason to get out of your place of refuge?

15. How would you encourage someone to leave their place of refuge?

16. Discuss three times in your life when you had to begin again.

17. What was the worst thing about beginning again?

18. What is the best thing about beginning again?

19. In your opinion, what is the key element of successfully beginning again?

_____

_____

_____

_____

_____

_____

_____

_____

20. How would you encourage someone to begin again?

We publish books, audios, and videos to help you feed His sheep.

Visit
ShelteringTreeMedia.com
for more information.

www.ingramcontent.com/pod-product-compliance
Lightning Source LLC
Chambersburg PA
CBHW032216040426
42449CB00005B/633